Tales from Grimm

retold by Ulla Dolt and
Geoffrey Summerfield

Ward Lock Educational

WARD LOCK EDUCATIONAL CO., LTD.
47 MARYLEBONE LANE,
LONDON W1M 6AX

A member of the Ling Kee Group
LONDON · HONG KONG · TAIPEI

TALES FROM GRIMM

ISBN 0 7062 3947 4 schools edition
ISBN 0 7062 3951 2 net edition

First published 1982

Series advisers:
Ralph Lavender and Dennis Saunders

PRINTED BY TOPMAN PRINTING PRESS LTD.

Ward Lock Educational Storyworld
General Editor: Geoffrey Summerfield

Tales from Grimm

Contents

6 **The Fox and the Cat**
Illustrated by Quentin Blake

8 **The Old Man and his Grandson**
Illustrated by Elaine Turney

10 **The Piece of Straw, the Piece of Coal and the Bean**
Illustrated by Gill Bradley

13 **The Wren and the Bear**
Illustrated by David Davies

18 **Doctor Know-All**
Illustrated by Elaine Turney

23 **Clever Gretel**
Illustrated by Susan Hellard

28 **The Singing Bone**
Illustrated by Lyn Bruce

33 **Old Sultan**
Illustrated by Andrzej Krauze

38 **Rebuses**
Illustrated by David Davies

40 **Fledgling**
Illustrated by Per Dahlberg

45 **The Queen Bee**
Illustrated by Carolyn Goudy

50 **The Little Mouse, the Little Bird and the Fried Sausage**
Illustrated by Quentin Blake

54 **The Fox and the Geese**
Illustrated by Tony Watson

56 **The Twelve Hunters**
Illustrated by David Sim

62 **Yorinde and Yoringel**
Illustrated by Josanne Cowell

68 **Sweet Porridge**
Illustrated by Per Dahlberg

70 **Fortune's Three Favourites**
Illustrated by Catherine Woolnough

76 **The Old Woman in the Woods**
Illustrated by Carolyn Goudy

The Fox and the Cat

One day the cat met the fox in the woods and because she thought he was not only clever but also important, she was very polite. 'Good afternoon, dear Mr Fox, and how are you today? How are you managing, in these hard times?'

The fox, who was very fond of himself, looked the cat up and down and wasn't at all sure that he could be bothered to reply. At last he said, 'Oh, you miserable face-washer, you patchwork fool, you skinny mouse-hunter! What's got into you? What gave you the idea that you could poke your nose into my affairs? What do you know that's of any importance? What can you do that's of any earthly use?'

'Well, I can do one thing for sure,' said the cat, modestly.

'And what, may I ask, is that?'

'When the dogs come, I can leap up into a tree and save my skin.'

'Is that all?' sneered the fox. 'Pooh, I can do hundreds of things. Why, I've got a whole bag of tricks. All I can say is, I'm sorry for you. So you'd better come along with me, and I'll teach you some useful lessons.'

At that very moment, along came a hunter with his four dogs. The cat nimbly sprang up into a tree and sat in the topmost branches, completely hidden by the leaves.

'Open your bag of tricks, Mr Fox,' shouted the cat. 'Open your bag!'

But the dogs already had the fox by the throat and held on to him tight.

'Ah, Mr Fox!' the cat called out. 'It looks as if you've come to the end of the road with your great bag of tricks. If only you'd had just one trick – to leap up into a tree – you wouldn't be getting your come-uppance!'

The Old Man and his Grandson

There was once an old man, as old as the hills. His eyes were dim, he was almost stone-deaf and his knees kept knocking. When he sat at the table at mealtimes he could hardly hold his spoon steady, and he would spill his soup on the tablecloth or have it dribbling down his chin.

His son and daughter-in-law were so disgusted with him that they put him at a table all alone, on the other side of the stove. They served his food in an earthenware bowl and never gave him a generous portion. So there he sat, just looking at the table, with tears in his eyes.

One day, his hands were so shaky that he dropped his bowl, which fell to the floor and smashed. His daughter-in-law gave him a good scolding, but all he did was to sigh a deep sigh. Then she bought him a cheap wooden bowl to eat out of.

One day, they were all eating their dinner, but the old man's grandson, who was about four, was playing on the floor, making a collection of pieces of wood.

'What are you up to?' his father asked.

'I'm building a little trough. When you and Mother grow old, you'll be able to eat out of it,' he replied.

Then his father and mother looked at each other for a long time without a word and then they started to weep. They went over to the old man and led him to their table where they gently sat him down.

From that day, he always ate his meals with them and they never said a word when he spilled his food.

The Piece of Straw, the Piece of Coal and the Bean

A poor old woman lived in a small village. One day, she gathered some beans to make herself a meal. First she lit a fire under the oven and, to get it going quickly, she put a handful of dry straw in the fireplace.

Then she put her beans in the pot, but one of them fell unnoticed onto the floor and came to rest by the side of a piece of straw. So there was a bean and a piece of straw tucked up snugly together on the floor.

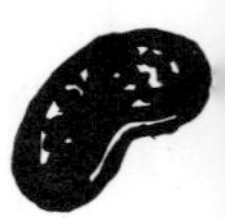

In no time, a piece of coal leapt out of the fire and landed by their side. And the straw said, 'Hello, you two! Where've you come from?'

The coal said, 'Well, I was very lucky. I was up there in the fire and, if I hadn't made a great effort to escape, I'd have been burnt to a cinder.'

The bean said, 'And I was lucky, too. If I'd ended up in the pot, I'd have been mashed to a pulp like all my mates.'

And the straw said, 'Do you think the same sort of thing would have happened to me? The old woman made all my pals go up in smoke! You should have seen her: sixty of them all snatched up at once and jammed into the fire! I was lucky to slip through her fingers and get out alive.'

'But what are we going to do now?' asked the piece of coal.

And the bean said, 'I think we should all stick together and be good friends. We are all lucky escapers, aren't we? Let's all emigrate together to a foreign country and keep out of harm's way.'

So the other two agreed, and they all set off together. Soon they came to a small brook and, as there was no sign of a bridge to get across, it looked as if they were stuck.

But the piece of straw said, 'I know. I'll stretch myself over the brook, from this side to that, then you can use me as a bridge.' So he stretched himself across the water.

Then the piece of coal set off across the narrow bridge of straw: he was really hot stuff and tiptoed onto the bridge without any hesitation. But when he got as far as the middle of the straw bridge, he heard the water in the brook gurgling and gulping and he was scared stiff. So he just stood there, petrified. And since he was still hot, he burned a hole in the straw, the straw burned through, broke in two, and fell – splash! – into the water. And the piece of coal went

tumbling down with him. Hiss! The coal hit the water, sank, and fizzled out.

All this time, the bean, who was a very careful fellow, stood on the bank of the stream and watched it all happen. And he burst out laughing when he saw the straw and coal fall into the water. He laughed and laughed till he burst! And there he was, burst in two!

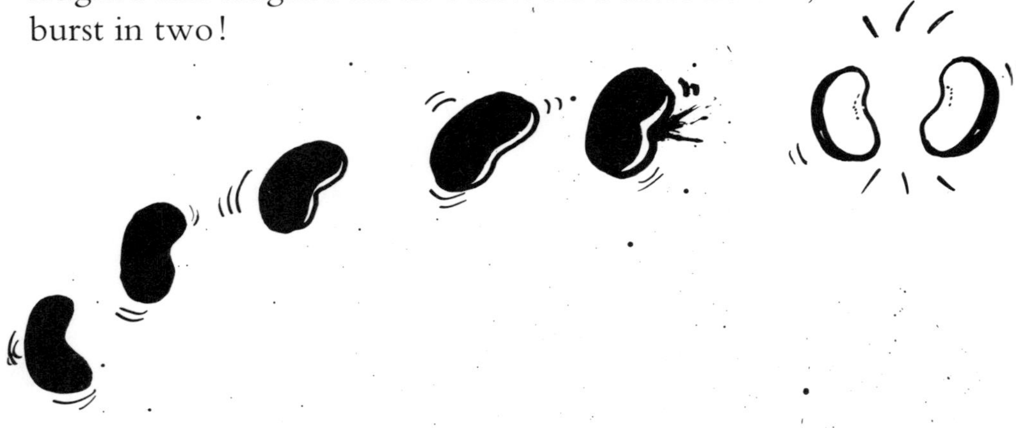

But, fortunately for him, a tailor happened to be going for a stroll, and was just having a rest nearby. He was a kind-hearted fellow and, when he saw that the poor bean was burst, he took out his needle and thread and stitched him together again.

'Thank you very, very, very much,' said the bean. And to this day if you look very closely, you'll see that all beans have a neat seam where the tailor sewed the bean together again.

The Wren and the Bear

One summer's day, a bear and wolf were walking through the woods.

Suddenly the bear heard a bird singing a beautiful tune, and said: 'Brother wolf, what bird is that?'

'It's the king of birds,' said the wolf. 'We must be very polite and respectful to him!' The wolf was joking, for it was really a wren that was singing. But the bear took it all seriously, and said, 'If it's the *king* of the birds, then he must live in a palace. And I would like to see it.'

'Not so easy,' said the wolf. 'In any case, we'll have to wait until the queen comes home.'

Soon, Jenny Wren came flying past with her mate, on their way to their nest, both carrying food in their beaks, to feed their young. The bear wanted to follow them, but the wolf grabbed him by the elbow and said, 'Not so fast! We must wait until they both go off on their travels again.'

So the bear made a note of exactly where the hole was where the wrens had built their nest, and then he and the wolf went off for a walk. But the bear was impatient to see the royal palace, and soon went back to have a look at the nest.

The wrens had flown off again, and he peeped into the hole and saw a small nest with five or six young birds in it.

'Is that the royal palace?' he cried. 'What a miserable little hole it is! And as for you pathetic little birds – you can't possibly be the king's

children! You're just pretending!'

When the young wrens heard the bear's insults, they were furious and yelled out, 'No, we're not! We're not miserable or pathetic! Our parents are very good people. They'll make you pay for your insults!'

The bear and the wolf took fright when they heard this threat, and sneaked off to their holes. But the young wrens in the nest went on screaming and making a fuss until their parents came back again. Then they all said, 'We're not going to eat a thing – not even a delicious fly's leg, until you've taught that silly bear that we are respectable people. As it is, he's just paid a visit and insulted us all.'

The father replied: 'Relax! Take it easy! We'll sort it out.' Then he and his wife flew to the bear's hole, and shouted, 'You old grumble-guts! What do you think you're up to, insulting our children? We'll make you pay for this. It's war, that's what it is, and blood will be shed!' Then they flew back to their nest.

So war was declared, and the bear went to see all the four-footed animals to get them to take his side: the ox, the cow, the ass, the stag, and every other creature with four feet. And the wren flew off to call all the birds to help: not only the birds, but all the creatures of the air – gnats, bees, flies and hornets.

When it was time to do battle, the wren decided to choose a scout to go and spy, to find out who was in charge of the four-footed army. The gnat, the most cunning of all the fliers, was given the job. She went silently into the wood where the four-footed army was gathering, and hid under a leaf on a tree where the four-footers were planning their battle. And she heard every word they said.

The bear told the fox to come forward, and said, 'Fox, you are the most cunning of all of us. So you must be our general and lead us into battle.'

'Good!' said the fox. 'But what is our signal going to be?'

Nobody had any idea, so the fox said, 'I have a beautiful long bushy tail. From a distance it looks like a great plume of red feathers. When you see me hold it up in the air, that means that we are doing well, and we must go on fighting until we gain a victory. But if I lower it to the ground, that means we are losing, and everybody must run for his life!'

The gnat heard every word, flew back to all the birds and other winged creatures, and told the wren

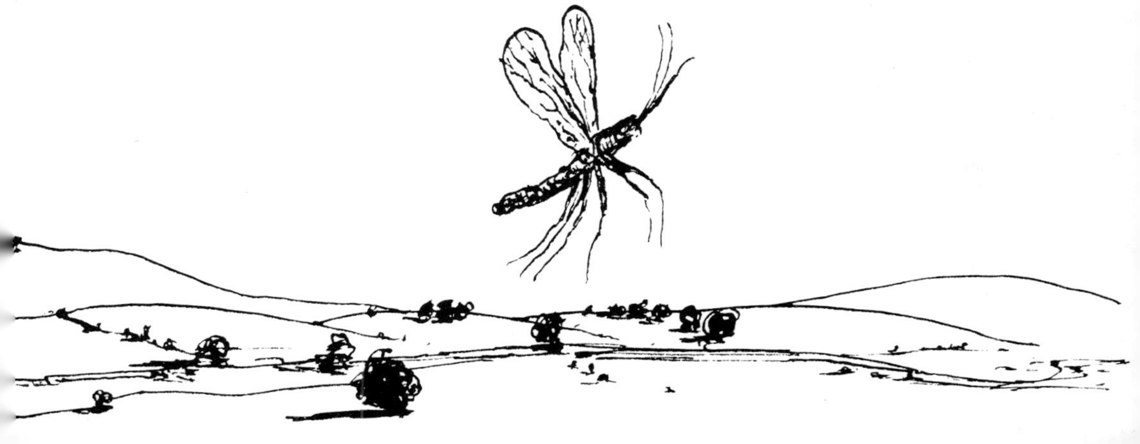

everything. Next day, at sunrise, the battle began. The four-footers all came rushing along, with such a hullabaloo that the ground trembled. And the wren with his army came zooming through the air, in the other direction, humming, crying and buzzing.

So the two armies met, and fought. Then the wren sent the hornet after the fox, and every time the fox stuck his tail up in the air, the hornet's job was to sting it so hard that the fox would pull his tail down. The hornet stung the fox once: the poor fox leapt in the air with the pain, but managed to keep his tail up. The hornet stung the fox a second time: and the

poor fox pulled his tail down for a second, then put it up again. The hornet stung the fox a third time and this time it was too much! The fox screamed out loud, tucked his tail between his legs, and ran for his life.

The four-footers saw him drop his tail and retreat, and came to the conclusion that they had already lost. So they all ran off in every direction, completely bewildered. And so the creatures of the air won the fight.

Then the wrens rushed back to their nest. 'Cheer up, children! Eat and drink as much as you like. We have won!'

But the young wrens wouldn't touch a thing. They all said, 'We'll not touch a thing, until the bear comes to apologize, and admits that were are respectable!'

So the father went to see the bear. 'Old grumbler, if you don't come this minute, and apologize to our children, I'll break every bone in your body!'

The poor bear was terrified! And he crawled to the nest, and said he was very sorry.

So the young wrens were finally satisfied, and they all tucked into their food and drink, and had a great time until it was time for them to go to bed.

Doctor Know-All

Once upon a time there was a poor farmer, Mr Krab. One day he drove a wagon-load of wood into town, and sold it to a doctor for two shillings. When he went into the house to be paid, the doctor was eating his dinner, and when poor Mr Krab saw how well the doctor lived, all his food and drink, the farmer wished that he had been a doctor and could live like that.

The doctor gave him the money, but Mr Krab just stood there, and at last he said, 'Do you think I could be a doctor?'

'Of course,' said the doctor. 'That's easy!'

'Is it?' said Mr Krab. 'How do I go about it?'

'First find yourself an ABC book, with a picture of a farmyard rooster in it. Then, sell your oxen and your wagon, and buy some respectable clothes, like mine. And finally, get somebody to paint a sign for you, with the words "Doctor Know-All" on it.'

So the farmer went home, and he did all this. After a while, a few patients came to see him, but not many.

And then the house of a rich man in the town was burgled. The rich man said he would pay a good reward to anyone who could catch the thief or get the stolen money back, and then someone told him about Doctor Know-All. Surely *he* would be able to find out who the thief was.

So the rich man went to visit him.

'Are you Doctor Know-All?'

'That's me,' said Mr Krab.

Then the rich man asked him to go with him to his great house, to solve the mystery of the burglary.

'I'll come willingly,' said Mr Krab, 'as long as I can bring my wife, Gretel, along with me.'

This was agreed, and they all set off in the rich man's carriage.

As soon as they reached the great house, the table was laid, and Mr Krab and his wife sat down ready to eat.

A servant came in and placed a dish of fine food on the table, and Mr Krab nudged his wife and said, 'Gretel, that's number one.'

He simply meant that this servant was only the first of many, because he wanted his wife to be impressed by the fact that they were the guests of a

rich man who employed a lot of servants. But the servant heard Mr Krab say, 'That's number one', and since he had been one of the burglars he thought that Mr Krab had recognized him. When he got back to the kitchen he said to his mates: 'That Doctor Know-All knows all about us! He just told his wife that I'm one of the thieves.'

The other servants were so scared, they hardly dared to go into the dining-room. But they had no choice. So one of them went in with the second course of the meal.

As he placed the food on the table, he saw Mr Krab nudge his wife and say, 'This is number two.' The poor fellow rushed back into the kitchen as fast as he could.

The same thing happened to the third servant. Krab said, 'Gretel, this is number three.'

The fourth servant had to carry in a covered dish, and the rich man asked 'Doctor Know-All' to show his skill and guess what was hidden in the dish, under the lid. In fact, the dish contained crabs.

Krab looked at the dish, and realized he was in quite a fix. He muttered, 'Krab, Krab, what are you going to do now?'

The rich man heard him mutter 'Krab' and said, 'There! Crab! He's right! He knows! So he'll know where my money is hidden!'

By this time, the servants were all worried stiff, and gave Mr Krab a nod and a wink, to get him to go outside and talk to them. Once outside, all four of them confessed that they were the thieves, and promised to return the money and to give Krab a reward if he would keep his mouth shut.

He agreed, on condition that they would take him to the place where they had hidden the money. This they did, and took him to the place straight away.

Then Mr Krab went back to the dining-room, sat down, and said, 'Sir, I will now see what my book has to tell me, then I will discover the money.'

A fifth servant, also one of the burglars, had hidden behind the stove, to listen carefully to see if Mr Krab knew any more about their goings-on. Doctor Know-All sat there, opened his ABC book, and turned the pages backwards and forwards, pretending to look for important information. And he grumbled: 'You must be in here somewhere! And you'd better come out!'

But the fifth man, hiding behind the stove, thought that Mr Krab was talking to him, and jumped out, scared stiff. 'This man knows everything!' he shouted.

Then Mr Krab took the rich man to the place where the money was hidden, but he never did tell anybody who had stolen it.

Clever Gretel

Once upon a time there was a cook by the name of Gretel. When she went out walking in her shoes with bright red heels, she minced and flounced this way and that, with a happy smile on her face, thinking, 'Goodness gracious me, but you are a pretty wench!'

When she got back to the house, she was feeling so pleased with herself that, for a treat, she helped herself to a glass of wine. Then the wine whetted her appetite, so she tucked into the best of the food on the cooker until she was full up. 'Well,' she said to herself, 'it's only common sense. When you're cooking a meal, you've got to find out what the food tastes like.'

One day, the man she worked for said, 'Gretel, I have a guest coming to supper this evening, so I want you to cook a couple of chickens. And be sure to make a really nice job of them!'

'Of course, sir!' said Gretel and she took the two best chickens and prepared them for cooking. She slit their throats, scalded them, plucked them and then, as the sun started to set, she put them on a spit in front of the fire, to roast. Soon they were done to a turn, nice and brown all over, but the guest hadn't arrived.

Gretel said, 'If your guest doesn't arrive soon, I'll have to take these chickens away from the fire. They're done to a turn and it's a pity I can't serve them straight away, while they are still so juicy.'

'I'll run out and fetch my guest,' said her boss and, as soon as he had left, Gretel put the chickens on one side and thought, 'Phew! Standing close by this roaring fire is hot work and I've worked up a great thirst. Who knows when they'll come to eat? I'll just nip down to the cellar and have a drop to drink.'

So she hurried downstairs, put the wine-jug to her lips, said, 'Bless you, Gretel!' and took a great swig. 'Wine should flow freely, and nobody should stop it,' she said, and took another great swig. Then she went back to the kitchen, put the chickens by the fire again, basted them with fresh butter and gave the spit a good spin. They smelt so delicious that she thought, 'I'd better check to see if they're properly cooked. I'll just have to taste a bit.' So saying, she did just that.

'Oh! What a marvellous chicken! What a crying shame that they have to sit around, waiting to be eaten!' She ran to the window, but there was no sign of her boss or of his guest, so she went back to the fire place.

'One of those wings is burning, I'm sure. A pity to let it burn. I'd better stop it.'

So she ate the wing, and then the chicken looked rather lop-sided. 'The boss is going to notice that something's missing. I'd better take the other one, to even things up.' So she ate the second wing, then she went to the window again but there was still no sign of anyone.

'Perhaps they're not going to come at all! Probably gone to a pub for a drink. Ah well, cheer up, Gretel. Go and help yourself to another drop of that wine, then finish that chicken off. And when it's all put away, you'll be able to rest content. God's good gifts shouldn't be wasted.' So she drank more of the wine and then polished off the rest of the chicken with no trouble at all.

There was still no sign of her boss and his guest, so Gretel took a good look at the second chicken. 'Where the one chicken has gone, the other one should go, as well. It's a shame to separate them. After all, what's sauce for the goose is sauce for the gander! And another drop of that wine won't hurt me, either!'

Just as she was picking the bones of her second chicken, who should she hear coming through the front door, but her boss! 'Hurry up with the meal, Gretel,' he shouted. 'My guest is coming along soon.'

'Yes, sir!' said Gretel. 'It'll be ready in no time.'

Then her boss went to make sure that the table was properly laid and took the great carving knife to sharpen it on the back door-step, so that he could make a good job of carving the chicken.

Just then, the guest knocked quietly at the front door. Gretel ran to open it, and when she saw who it was, she put her finger to her lips and said, 'Don't make a sound! If he gets hold of you, it'll be all the worse for you. Sure enough, he invited you to supper, but do you know what he's going to do? Cut your ears off! Listen – that's him sharpening his knife!'

Gretel then left the guest to make off as fast as he could and, wasting not a second, she ran through to the back door and said to the boss, 'That was a ridiculous guest you invited to supper!'

'Why, Gretel? What's the matter?'

'He snatched both the chickens off the dish, just as I was going to serve them up, and he's run off with them!'

'Well, I never! That's a fine way to carry on!' He was very sorry to have lost both his chickens. 'He might at least have left me one, then I wouldn't have to go without my supper.'

So he called after his guest, begging him to stay, but the poor fellow pretended not to hear a thing and just went on running. Then he ran after him – his carving knife was still flashing in his hand! – shouting out, 'Just one! I only wanted one!'

But his poor guest thought he was talking about ears, and ran and ran, lifting up his feet like a cat on hot bricks. He was determined to get home with his two ears still safe and sound, on his head where they belonged.

The Singing Bone

Once there was a country where the people were all very unhappy because a great wild boar was tearing around the place. It was digging up all the crops in the fields, and chasing the cows, and even hurting people with its terrible sharp tusks.

One day the King offered a reward: 'A BIG REWARD FOR ANYONE WHO CAN GET RID OF THE TERRIBLE BOAR.' But it was no good. The boar was so big and strong that nobody even dared to go anywhere near the woods where it lived. So finally the King announced a special reward. 'IF ANY MAN CAN CATCH OR KILL THE BOAR, HE CAN MARRY MY DAUGHTER, THE PRINCESS.'

A poor man had two sons and when they heard about the King's offer, they both wanted to try to win the reward. The older son was a real big-head and clever and cunning. His younger brother was a simple lad and he wanted to have a go because he wanted to do everybody a favour.

So, there was the terrible boar in the middle of the wood and the King told the brothers to go into the wood from opposite sides so that they would have a better chance of finding the boar. The older brother went in from the west and the younger one went in from the east.

The younger brother hadn't walked very far through the wood before a little man appeared, carrying a small black spear. And he said, 'I'll give you this spear, because you are a good lad. As long as you hold this spear, you can go right up to that wild boar and he won't be able to hurt you.'

The young brother thanked the little man, put the spear over his shoulder, and went on into the dark wood, without any fear. After a while, he saw the wild boar, which came charging at him. He held the spear very firm and pointed it at the boar, which ran so hard onto the spear that its heart was cut in two and it lay dead. The young brother then put the beast over his shoulder to carry it off to the King.

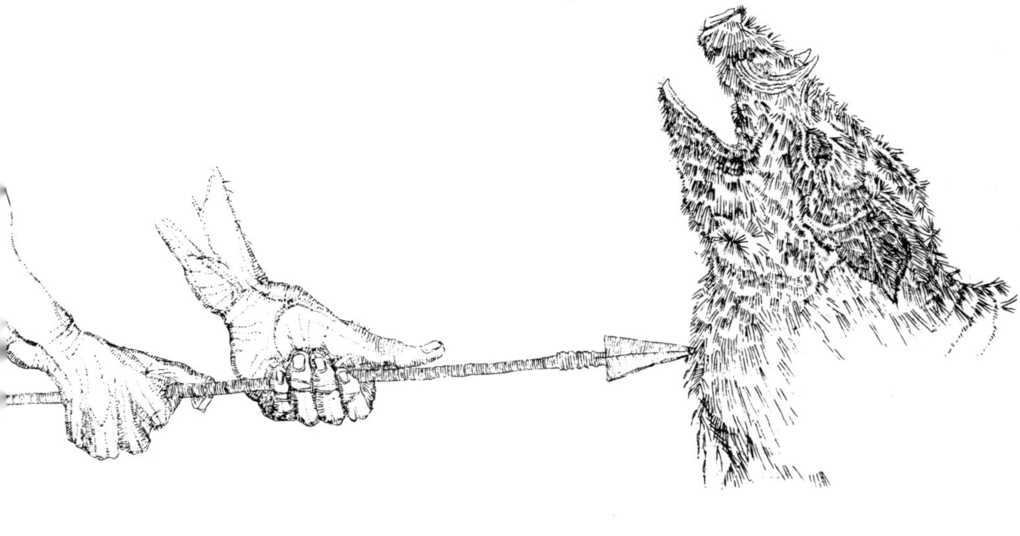

But when he reached the other side of the wood he came to a house where all the people were enjoying themselves, dancing, drinking and laughing. And there was his older brother who was drinking to build up his courage before he went into the wood to meet the boar. When he saw his young brother come out of the wood, carrying the dead boar on his shoulders, he was full of envy and jealousy. But he pretended to be pleased. 'Come in, brother, and have a rest and a refreshing drink of wine.'

The younger brother didn't think he would come to harm, so he went in. Then he told his brother about what had happened – all about the little man and the spear and how he had killed the boar.

The older brother kept him talking till it was dark and then they left the house together. They went off in the dark and came to a bridge across a stream.

'You go first,' said the older brother.

When the young lad reached the middle of the bridge, his brother hit him from behind on the head and he fell dead into the water.

Then the older brother buried him under the bridge, picked up the wild boar and took it to the King. He pretended that he had killed the beast and of course the King gave him his reward and he married the King's daughter.

When his younger brother failed to turn up, he said, 'The wild boar must have killed him and torn him to shreds.' And everybody believed him. But nothing is hidden forever, and one day his crime came to light.

Many years later, a shepherd was driving his flock of sheep across the bridge. He saw something shining in the sand by the stream. He went to pick it up, and it was a bright white bone.

'I can carve this to make a good mouthpiece for my horn,' he said to himself.

So he shaped the bone and fixed it to his horn. But he was amazed when the bone began to sing its own tune.

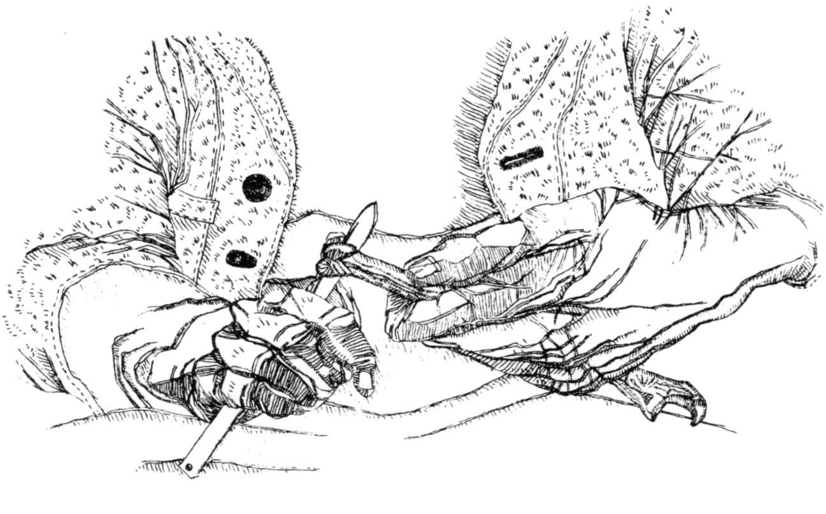

'Oh shepherd, standing all alone,
Hear the singing of my bone!
On this bridge my brother killed me,
In this stream he buried me,
To claim the wild boar's slaughter
And claim the King's own daughter.'

'What a funny little horn that can sing all by itself! I must go and show it to the King!'

When he reached the King's palace, the little horn began to sing again. Straightaway, the King knew what the song meant and he had the soil dug up near the bridge. The skeleton of the younger brother was uncovered.

The older brother now couldn't deny his crime, so he was sewn up in a large sack and thrown into the river to drown. And the younger brother's skeleton was laid to rest in a beautiful grave in the churchyard.

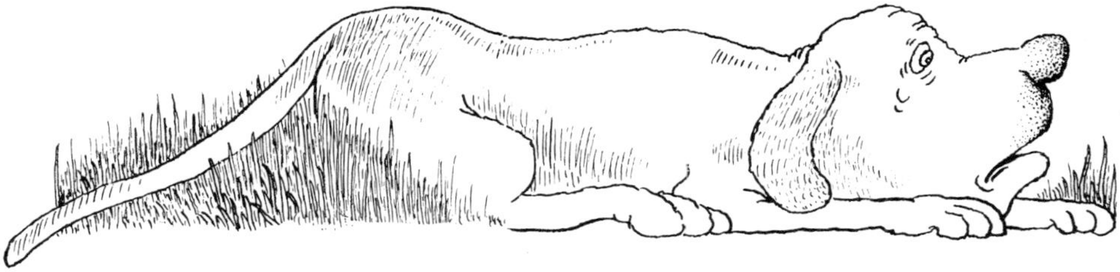

Old Sultan

A farmer once had a faithful dog whose name was Sultan. When the dog was old, he lost all his teeth and couldn't grip anything with his mouth.

One day, the farmer and his wife were standing by their front door and the farmer said, 'Tomorrow I'm going to shoot Old Sultan. He's really good for nothing now'.

But his wife felt sorry for the faithful old dog and said, 'He has worked well for us, for a long time now; he's been a good dog and I think we should be kind to him.'

'Nonsense!' said the farmer. 'Don't be so silly. He hasn't got a single tooth left in his head and there's not a thief that's afraid of him. It's time he was put down. Of course he's served us well, but we fed him well in return.'

The poor dog, who was quite close by, stretched out in the sunlight, heard what they were saying and was very sad when he learned that the next day might be his last.

So that night he went off to the woods to see his old friend, the wolf, and he told him all the terrible news of his approaching death.

'Now, listen to me, old friend,' said the wolf. 'Cheer up, and I'll help you to get out of this trouble. Now, I've got an idea. Tomorrow, early in the morning, the farmer and his wife are going out to the fields to cut their hay. And they'll have to take their little baby with them because nobody's going to stay behind in the house. While they're working in the field, they usually put the baby behind the hedge out of the sun. Now you must go and lie down by the baby, as if you were guarding it. Then I'll sneak out of the woods and snatch the baby up. You must leap at me and bark angrily as if you were trying to take the baby away from me. Then I'll drop it and you can carry it back to its parents. They'll believe that you've saved its life and they'll be far too pleased and thankful to do you any harm. Quite the opposite! They'll not only spare your life but they'll do all they can to make you comfortable: you'll be able to live in the lap of luxury.'

Old Sultan liked the wolf's plan and next day it all worked like clockwork. When the farmer saw the wolf running off with the baby in his mouth, he screamed like mad. But when Old Sultan brought the child back, the farmer was delighted and patted the dog and said, 'We'll not hurt a hair on your head! We're going to spoil you with kindness and give you everything you need.'

Then the farmer said to his wife, 'Hurry off home and mix some bread and milk for Old Sultan. And take the pillow off my bed. He can have it in his corner, to rest his head on.'

So Old Sultan was as comfortable as he could ever have hoped for.

Soon the wolf visited Old Sultan and said he was very glad that everything had turned out so well.

'Now, old mate,' the wolf said, 'I hope you'll turn a blind eye when I help myself to one of your boss's fat sheep now and again. In these days, it's difficult to make ends meet.'

'Don't bank on that,' the dog answered. 'I must serve my master. So you can't expect me to agree to your plan.'

The wolf didn't believe that Old Sultan really meant what he said, so he crept out by night to steal

a sheep. But the dog had told the farmer about the wolf's plans, so the farmer was lying in wait for the wolf and when he caught him he gave him a good hiding.

As the wolf ran away he shouted back at the dog, 'You just wait! You mean dog! You'll pay for this!'

Next morning, the wolf sent the wild boar to challenge the dog to come out to the woods to settle the argument. Poor Old Sultan couldn't find anybody to help him, except for a cat with only three legs, who agreed to go along with him.

As they went together to the woods, the cat went limping along on its three legs and held its tail high in the air because it was sore. The wolf and the boar were waiting for them, but when they saw Old Sultan and his friend coming through the wood they thought he was going to come and cut them to pieces with a sword. They mistook the cat's raised tail for a sword!

And when they saw the cat limping along on its three legs they mistook it for somebody bending down to pick up a handful of pebbles to pelt them with. And they were so scared that the boar went to hide behind the leaves and the wolf went scrambling up a tree. So, when Old Sultan and the cat reached the place for the meeting they were surprised to find nobody there. But the wild boar hadn't made a very good job of hiding himself and his ears were still sticking out.

The cat decided to have a good look around and he saw the boar's ears twitching. He mistook the twitching ears for a mouse stirring in the leaves, so

he leapt at them and gave them a sharp bite. Then the boar sprang out from behind the leaves, and screamed, and made a terrible hullabaloo. 'Over there!' he shouted. 'Up the tree! There's the culprit.'

Old Sultan and the cat looked up into the tree and saw the wolf. And the wolf was so ashamed of himself that he came down and was pleased to agree when Old Sultan said, 'Let's be friends again.'

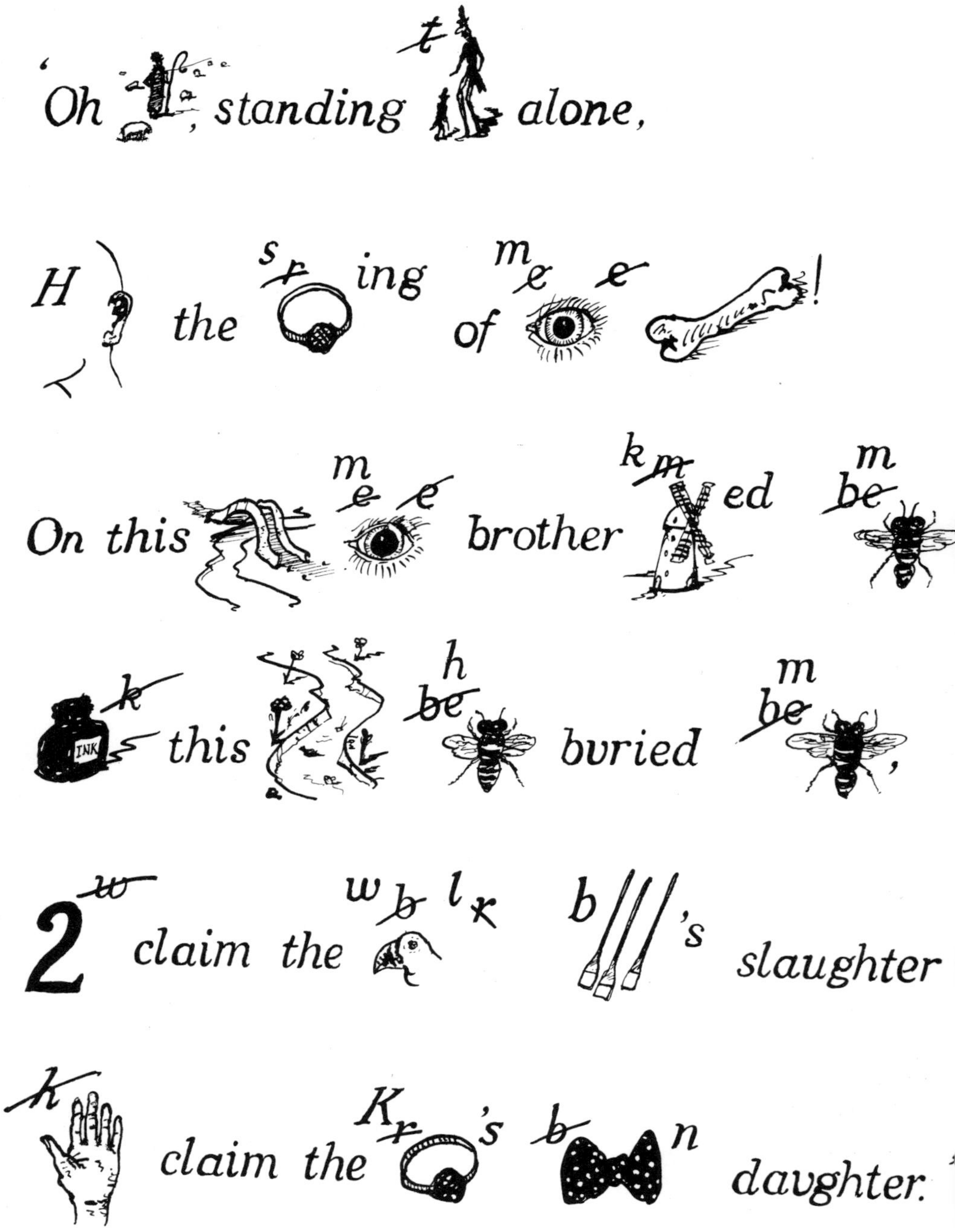

See page 32 for the answer

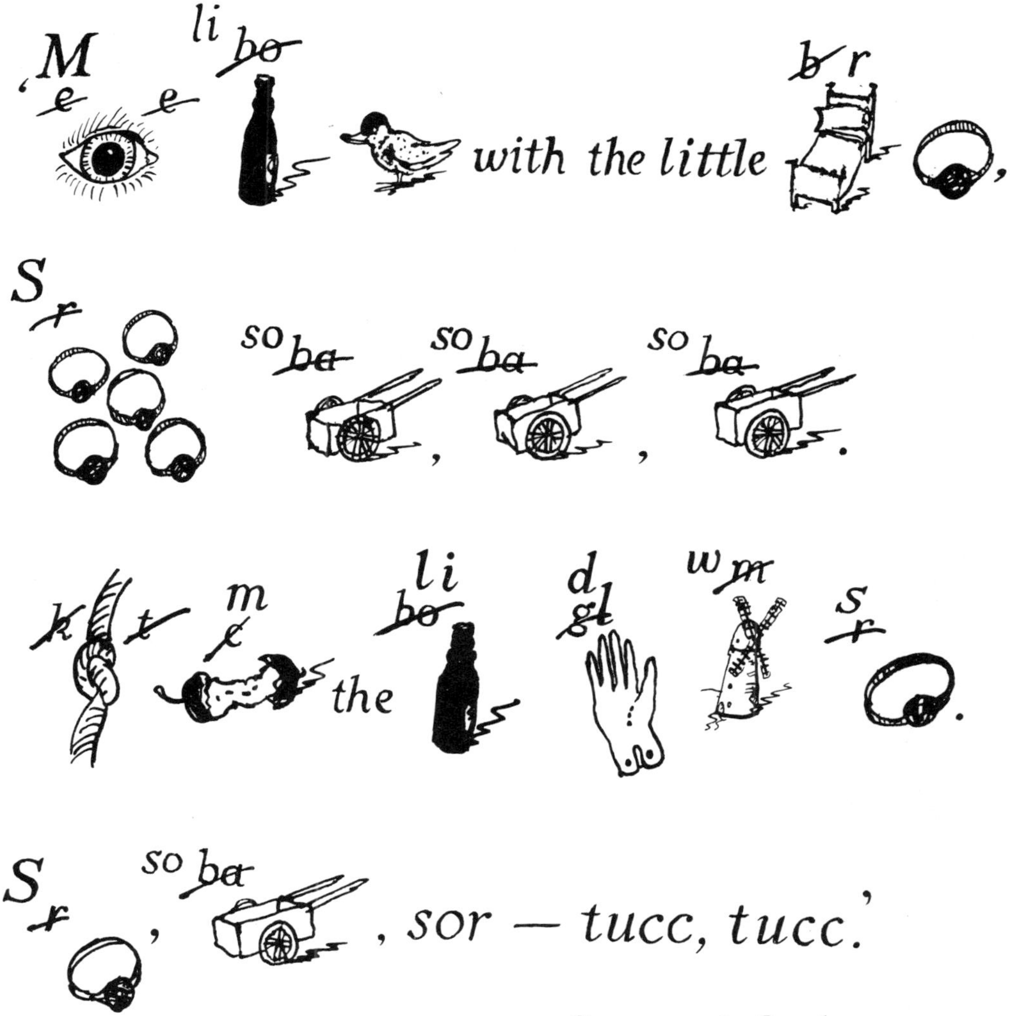

See page 64 for the answer

Fledgling

Once upon a time a forester went into the woods to hunt. As he was going into the woods he heard a noise that sounded like a baby crying. He followed the sound until he finally came to a tall tree. In the top of the tree, lo and behold, there was a baby.

The baby and his mother had fallen asleep in the shade of the tree and a great bird had seen the baby sleeping in the mother's arms. It had flown down and snatched the baby away in its beak and placed it in the top of the tree.

The forester climbed the tree and carried the baby down. He thought, 'I'll take the child home and bring it up with my daughter, Little Lena.'

So he took it home and the two children grew up together. And because the baby in the tree had been stolen by a bird he called it 'Fledgling', like a young bird in the nest before it can fly.

Fledgling and Little Lena loved each other so much that they never wanted to be parted. But the forester had an old cook and one evening she took two buckets and began to carry water from the well. She went to the well again and again and again.

When Little Lena saw her, she said, 'Listen, Old Susanna! Why are you fetching such a lot of water?'

The old woman replied, 'If you promise not to breathe a word to anybody, I'll tell you.'

Lena promised to keep the secret and Old Susanna then said, 'Tomorrow morning, while the forester is out hunting, I'm going to heat the water in a big pot

and when it's boiling, I'll throw Fledgling into the water and cook him!'

Next day, almost before it was light, the forester went out hunting. When he left, the children were still in bed and Lena said to Fledgling, 'If you'll never leave me, I'll never leave you.'

'Now and never,' Fledgling answered.

Then Lena said, 'I've got something to tell you. Yesterday old Susanna lugged ever so many buckets of water into the house. So I asked her what she was up to. When I promised to keep her secret, she told me that she was going to boil the water and cook you, while father was out hunting. Let's get up quickly, and get dressed, and run away.'

So the two children leapt out of bed, dressed themselves quickly and ran off.

Now, when the water in the pot came to the boil, Old Susanna went to the bedroom to fetch Fledgling and throw him in. But when she went in and shuffled close to the beds she saw that the children had gone. Then she was terribly frightened and muttered to herself, 'What am I going to say when the boss comes home and finds out that the children have gone? I must find somebody to go and search for them and bring them back.'

So she sent three farmhands to search for the children. But Lena and Fledgling were resting at the edge of the woods and when they saw the three farmhands in the distance, running towards them, Lena said, 'If you'll never leave me, I'll never leave you.'

And Fledgling answered, 'Now and never.'

Then Lena said, 'You must turn into a rose-bush. And I'll be the little rose growing on it.'

When the three farmhands reached the woods they found nothing but a rose-bush with one rose on it. The children were nowhere to be seen. So

they said, 'We've done all we can,' and went back to the farmhouse. There they told Old Susanna that they had seen nothing except a little rose-bush with one rose on it.

'You fools!' the old cook scolded. 'You should have cut the rose-bush in two and plucked the rose and brought it back here. Hurry, now, and go and do as I say.'

So the three farmhands went back to the woods, but the children saw them coming.

Lena said, 'Fledgling, if you'll never leave me, I'll never leave you.'

And Fledgling answered, 'Now and never.'

Then Lena said, 'Now, you must turn into a church and I will be the crown inside.'

So, when the three farmhands reached the woods, there was nothing but a church and a crown in it. So they said to each other: 'What can we do now? Let's go back.'

Again, Old Susanna asked them, 'Did you find them?'

But they answered, 'Only a church with a crown in it.'

'You idiots!' she shouted. 'Why didn't you destroy the church and bring the crown back here?'

Then the old woman roused herself and took the men to look for the children once again. But at a safe distance the children saw the three men running towards them, with Old Susanna tottering after them.

Lena said, 'If you will never leave me, I will never leave you.'

And Fledgling replied, 'Now and never.'

Lena said, 'Turn yourself into a pond, and I will be the duck swimming on it.'

When Old Susanna reached the pond she knelt down and she was just about to drink up all the water in the pond. But the duck swam quickly at her, grabbed her head in its beak and tugged her into the water. So the old witch drowned.

Then the two children went home together, as pleased as Punch. And if they haven't died, they are still living there!

The Queen Bee

One day two princes went out to look for some adventure. They got onto the wrong road and fell into a really wild way of living and never even bothered to go back home.

The youngest brother, who was called 'Blockhead', set off in search of them. But when at last he found the princes, they just poked fun at him and said, 'Just fancy! You, the blockhead, thinking you could find the right road through life! While we, who are much cleverer than you, couldn't find it!'

Then all three of them set off together and they came to an ant-hill. The two older brothers wanted to dig it up to watch the ants running about in sheer panic and trying to drag their eggs to safety.

But Blockhead said, 'Leave the poor creatures in peace. I'll not let you spoil their nest!'

So they went on until they reached a lake with lots of ducks swimming on it. The two older brothers wanted to catch some of them and roast them. But Blockhead wouldn't let them and said, 'Leave them in peace. I'll not let you kill them.'

At last, they came to a bee's nest. The honey in the nest was so plentiful that it was dripping all over the branches of the tree. The two older brothers wanted to light a fire beneath the tree to smoke the bees out, so that they could then steal the honey. But Blockhead again prevented them and said, 'Leave them in peace. I'll not allow you to burn them.'

Finally, the three brothers came to a castle where there were lots of stone horses standing in the stables. But there was not a single human being to be seen anywhere. They went through all the rooms, until they came to a door at the very end, with three locks.

In the middle of the door there was a little peephole and through this hole they could see into the next room. There they saw a little grey man sitting at a table. They shouted to him, once, twice. But he didn't seem to hear a thing. So they called a third time and he got up, unlocked the door, and came out.

He said not a word, but he led them to a beautiful table, laden with all manner of rich food. So they sat down and ate and drank and when they were full he guided each of them to a separate bedroom.

Next morning, the little grey man came to the eldest brother, gave him a sign and took him to a stone board. Written on the board were three tasks. If someone performed all of the tasks, then the spell would be lifted from the castle.

The first task was as follows: in the woods, beneath the moss, there lay a thousand pearls, belonging to a princess. They all had to be picked up

bzzzz
whats going on?
wait stop!

and if even a single pearl was not picked up by sunset, then he who performed the task would be turned to stone.

The eldest son went into the woods and searched all day long. But when it grew dark he had only found a hundred of the pearls. So the words written on the stone board came true and he was turned to stone.

Next day, the second brother accepted the challenge but he didn't do much better than the eldest. He didn't find more than two hundred pearls and so at sunset he was turned to stone.

At last it was Blockhead's turn and he went searching for pearls in the moss. But it was very difficult for him to find the pearls. In fact he got on so slowly that he finally sat down on a stone and wept. But while he was sitting there, crying, the king of the ants, whose life Blockhead had once saved, arrived and he brought with him an army of five thousand ants.

In no time at all, the ants had found all the pearls and collected them together in a heap.

The second task for Blockhead was to find the key to the princess's room; the key was somewhere at the bottom of the lake. But when he reached the water's edge, he met the ducks he had once saved and they all went diving to the bottom of the lake and finally came up with the key.

The third task was the most difficult. The king had three sleeping daughters and Blockhead had to say which of them was the youngest. They were so much alike that the only difference between them

was that before going to sleep they had eaten different sweets. The eldest had eaten a lump of sugar, the second a spoonful of syrup and the youngest a spoonful of honey. Then the queen of the bees, that Blockhead had saved from being burnt, came and tasted the lips of all three. And she stayed on the mouth of the youngest princess. This finally broke the spell so that everybody was released from sleep. Even those who had been turned to stone came alive again. Then Blockhead married the youngest and dearest princess, his brothers married the other two and they all lived happy lives.

The Little Mouse, the Little Bird and the Fried Sausage

Once upon a time a little mouse, a little bird and a fried sausage decided to live together. For a long time they were very happy and peaceful and they didn't go short of anything.

The little bird's job was to fly into the woods each day to collect firewood. The mouse fetched the water, lit the fire and laid the table. And the fried sausage cooked the meals.

But even those who have everything are never satisfied, and one day the little bird was flying about when he met another bird and told him all about his good life. But the other bird pooh-poohed his story. 'What a poor wretch you are! Just fancy, having to rush about looking for firewood while the other two are just lazing around at home.'

As a matter of fact, when the mouse had lit the fire and fetched the water it did manage to snatch a rest until it was time to lay the table. And the fried

sausage just stayed near the oven to make sure the meal was cooking properly and then, when mealtime came, it wriggled like greased lightning through the porridge or the broth and in no time at all the soup was greased, salted and ready.

When the little bird reached home, it put its load of wood down and joined the others at the table. When they had finished their meal, they all went to bed and slept like a log until next day. Altogether, it was a marvellous life!

But because of what the other bird had said, the little bird refused to go into the woods next day. 'I've been your servant long enough,' he said, 'and a real muggins. It's time we tried another way of running the house.'

The mouse and the sausage both pleaded with the bird to keep everything as it was, but it was no good. The bird put his foot down, so they agreed to try a change. They drew lots to see who would do what. The sausage drew the shortest straw, so he had to fetch firewood. The mouse became the cook. And the bird's job was to go for the water.

So what happened then? The sausage went marching off to the woods, the bird lit the fire and the mouse put the saucepan on the oven. And the bird and the mouse waited for a long time for the sausage to come back with the firewood. But he didn't return and soon they started to worry about him.

So the bird flew off to look for him and before long he met a dog on the road. Now, this dog had seen the sausage going to the woods and had decided that he was very easy prey. So he had leapt on him, knocked him down and finished him off.

'But how could you do such a thing?' the bird cried bitterly.

'It's no use crying,' said the dog. 'That sausage was up to no good. I was quite right to do him in.'

There was nothing the bird could do about it, so he picked up his firewood and went home, to tell the mouse what had happened.

They both felt very upset, but decided to make the best of a bad job and carry on as usual. So the bird laid the table and the mouse prepared the meal. Just before he served the broth, the mouse went wriggling through it to put some grease in it, just as the sausage used to do. But before he got to the middle of the saucepan, he drowned.

Then the bird came in to serve the meal. But where was the cook? Nowhere to be seen! So the bird threw the firewood down, shouted for the mouse and looked all over the room, but could find no trace of him.

And then the flames of the fire reached the firewood that the bird had thrown down so carelessly and in no time at all there was a great blaze. The bird went rushing out to the well, to get some water, but the bucket was too heavy and fell back down the well, pulling the bird after it. So the bird was drowned.

And that was the end of the little mouse, the little bird and the fried sausage.

The Fox and the Geese

One day, a fox came to a meadow where a flock of lovely fat geese were grazing. He laughed out loud and said, 'I've arrived just in the nick of time! Here you all are sitting together so tidily, I can eat you up one after the other.'

The geese all cackled with terror, leapt up for fear of their lives and begged to be spared. But the fox wouldn't listen to their pleadings and said, 'You must all die! There'll be no mercy.'

Finally, one of the geese plucked up her courage and said, 'If we poor geese have to sacrifice our young and healthy lives, at least allow us one favour and let us just pray for the peace of our souls. Then we will all stand in line, so that you can choose the fattest.'

'Very well,' said the fox. 'That's a decent enough request. So get on with your praying and I'll just wait until you've finished.'

Then the first goose started to cackle: 'Ga! Ga! Ga!' and before she'd finished, the second started too: 'Ga! Ga! Ga!' Then the third, and the fourth, and soon they were all cackling their prayers. And as soon as they have finished, we can get on with our story.

The Twelve Hunters

Once upon a time there was a prince who was very happy. He was looking forward to being married to the woman he loved more than anyone else in the world.

One day as they were sitting side by side, happy to be together, news arrived that the prince's father was very ill and wished to see his son before he died.

'I must go now to my father and leave you,' the prince said to his beloved, 'but I want you to take this ring to remember me by. If my father dies and I become king in his place, the first thing I'll do is to come back here and then I'll take you home.'

Then he rode away. And when he came to his father's bedside, he found that the king was very near to death. And the old man said, 'My dearest son, I wanted to see you once more before I died. I now want you to promise that you will marry the woman I have chosen for you.' Then the king named a certain princess who he had decided should marry his son.

The prince was so sad that he didn't think about what he was saying, but just blurted out, 'Yes, dear father, I will do whatever you wish.' And then the old king closed his eyes and died.

When the prince was proclaimed king and the time of mourning was over, he then had to keep the promise that he had made to his father. So it was arranged that the princess his father had named should be asked to marry him.

When his first love heard about this, she grieved so deeply over his broken promises that she almost died. Then her father said to her, 'My dear child, why are you so sad? Name whatever you want and your wish shall be granted.'

She thought for a moment and then said, 'Dear father, I wish for eleven girls who look exactly like me in every way.'

Her father said, 'If it's possible, your wish shall be granted,' and he had all the kingdom searched until eleven girls were found, who were exactly like his daughter in every way.

When they were brought to the princess, she had twelve hunters' costumes made, all alike, and all twelve girls put them on. Then the princess said goodbye to her father and rode away with the eleven girls.

She rode straight to the court of the man she loved and asked him if he needed twelve hunters in his service. The young king looked at her, but didn't recognize her, and the twelve hunters were so handsome that he said, 'Yes, I will take you all into my service,' so they became the twelve hunters of the king.

Now the king had a pet lion, which was a strange beast because it could see through every secret and mystery. One evening the lion said to the king, 'You think you have twelve hunters in your service?'

'Yes,' answered the king, 'they are indeed twelve hunters.'

But the lion replied, 'You are mistaken. They are twelve girls!'

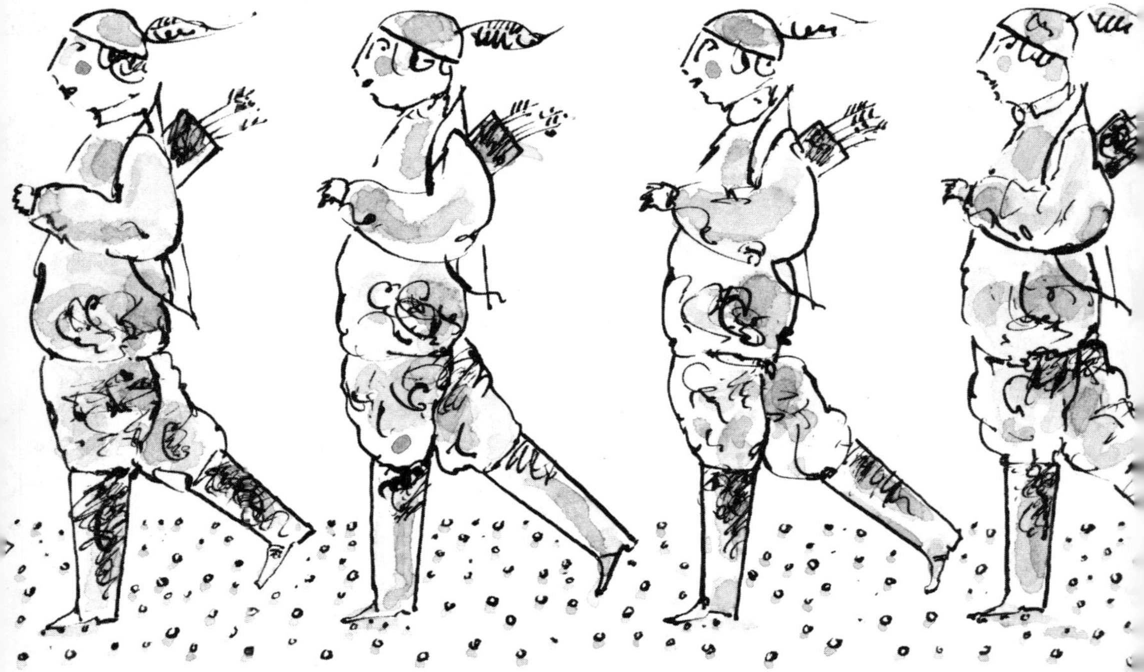

'That's ridiculous!' the king snapped. 'How do you intend to prove you are right?'

'Oh, just have some dried peas scattered on the floor in the next room,' the lion suggested, 'and you'll see I'm right. Men have a firm step. When they stride over the peas, not one is moved. But women tiptoe and pitter-patter, and shuffle their feet, and they send the peas flying in all directions.'

The king was pleased with the lion's advice and had peas strewn on the floor of the room. But one of the king's servants was very fond of the hunters and when he overheard the lion's advice he went to them and told them everything he had heard. 'Would you believe it! The lion is trying to make the king believe that you are really girls!'

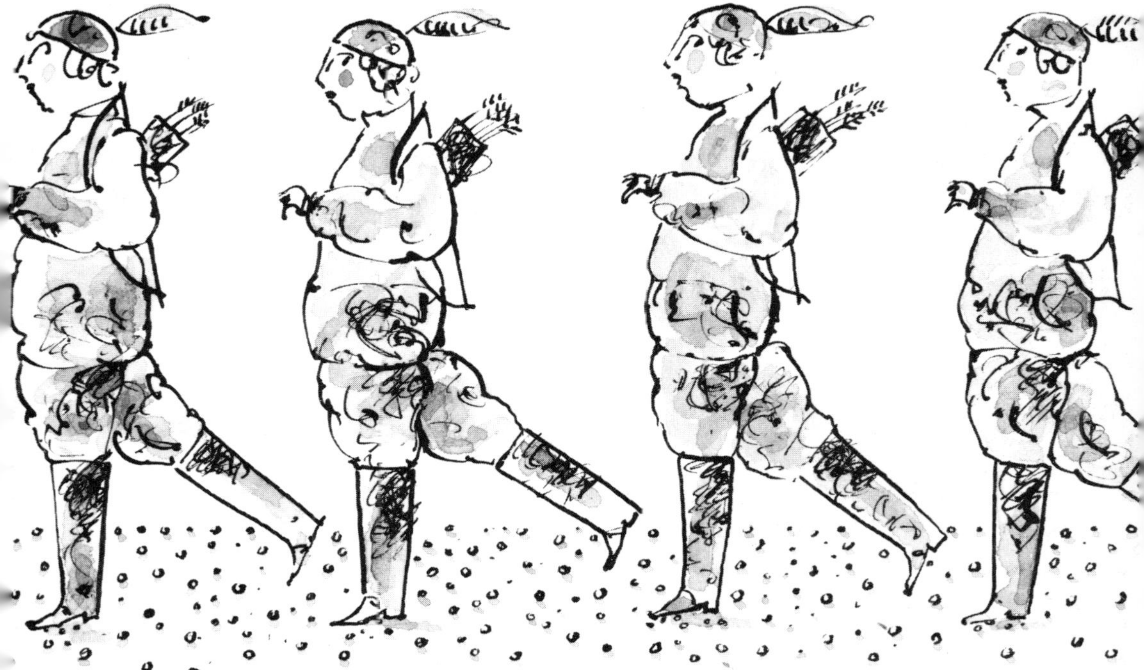

The princess thanked him for his news and said to the eleven girls, 'Now, take a firm grip on yourselves and bring your feet down on the dried peas very hard.'

Next morning, the king called for the twelve hunters and when they entered the room where the peas were scattered they stepped so firmly on them and had such a steady way of walking that not even one pea so much as rolled or moved. Then they were sent away again and the king said to the lion, 'You got it all wrong. They walked just like men.'

'Ah,' said the lion, 'they knew they were going to be tested, so they made a great effort not to be caught out. But you just have twelve spinning-wheels brought into the room and then see what happens. They'll all come crowding round them and touch them. And no man would do such a thing.'

The king was pleased with this advice and so he had twelve spinning-wheels placed in the room. But again the servant who wanted to be fair to the hunters went and told them of the plan. When they were alone, the princess said to the eleven girls, 'Keep a firm control over yourselves. And don't so much as peep at the spinning-wheels.'

Next morning, when the king called for his twelve hunters they went striding across the room and didn't even peep at the spinning-wheels.

And again the king said to the lion, 'You have told me a lie. They didn't even peep at the spinning-wheels, so they must be men.'

And the lion answered again, 'They knew that they were on trial and so they controlled themselves very hard.' But the king no longer believed the lion.

The twelve hunters always went with the king whenever he went out hunting, and the more he saw of them the more he liked them. But one day when they were all out hunting it happened that a messenger came to the king with the news that his bride-to-be, chosen by his father, was on her way to his court.

When his first love heard this, her heart almost broke and she fell to the ground in a faint. The king thought something was wrong with his favourite hunter and ran to help him. He drew off the hunter's glove and there on the finger he saw the ring which he had given to his first love. Then he looked closely at her face and recognized her.

His heart was so deeply moved that he kissed her and, when she opened her eyes, he said, 'You are mine and I am yours and no one in the world can alter that.'

Then he sent a messenger to the princess of his father's choosing and told her that he had already found the woman he wanted to marry. And she returned to her own kingdom. Those who have found their old key again, don't need a new one.

And so the wedding was celebrated and the poor old lion was once again in the king's good books, because now it was clear that he had been telling the truth all along.

Yorinde and Yoringel

There was once an old castle in the middle of a deep dark forest. An old woman lived there all alone and she was a great witch. By day she turned into a cat or a screech-owl but by night she became once again a human being. She had the power to get deer and birds to come to her and then she killed them and boiled or roasted them.

If anybody came within a hundred paces of the castle her spells made him stand still, rooted to the spot, and he couldn't move an inch until she released him from the spell. But if a young girl came into the witch's circle, she was turned into a bird and locked in a wicker cage. Then the old woman carried the cage into one of the rooms of the castle. She already had about seven thousand of these cages in her castle and each of them had a rare bird inside.

Now, there was a young girl called Yorinde, who was the most beautiful girl of all. She had promised to marry a handsome young man named Yoringel. They were already engaged and were very happy together. One day they wanted to talk without anybody else hearing them, so they went walking into the forest to be alone.

'We must be careful not to go too near to the castle,' said Yoringel. It was a beautiful evening and the setting sun shone brilliantly between the trees of the dark green wood. And the turtle doves were singing their sad songs in the old beech trees.

Yorinde and Yoringel stopped and looked around

them. They had lost their way and had no idea which was the way home. Yorinde wept now and then, sat down in the light of the setting sun and lamented. Yoringel also was upset. They were as sad as if they were about to die.

The sun was now halfway above the top of the hill, and halfway below. Yoringel peeped through the bushes and saw the old walls of the castle very close by. He was shocked and felt a terrible fear in his heart.

Yorinde was singing:

'My little bird with the little red ring,
Sings sorrow, sorrow, sorrow.
No more the little dove will sing.
Sing sorrow, sor – tucc, tucc.'

Yoringel looked about for Yorinde. She had turned into a nightingale and was singing, 'Tucc, tucc. Tucc, tucc.' Then a screech-owl with burning eyes flew round them three times and screeched three times: 'Eech, eech, eech.'

Yoringel couldn't move an inch. He stood there, like a stone. He couldn't weep. He couldn't speak. He could move neither hands nor feet.

By now the sun had set. The owl flew into a bush and soon after a crooked old woman came shuffling out, yellow and withered, with large red eyes and a hooked nose, its tip touching her chin. She was mumbling to herself, then she snatched the nightingale and took it away in her hand. Yoringel was dumbstruck. Nor could he move an inch. The nightingale had disappeared.

At last the old woman came back and cast a spell in a strange hollow voice:

'Greetings to you, Zachiel! When the moon shines on the cage, release him, Zachiel, at the right moment!'

Then Yoringel was freed from the spell. He fell to his knees in front of the old woman and begged her to let Yorinde go free. But she said, 'You'll never get her back,' and then she shuffled off. Yoringel shouted, wept, and moaned, but it was all in vain. 'Oh, what will become of me?' he cried.

Finally, he left the dark wood and came to a strange village. There, for a long time, he worked as a shepherd. And often he went and walked round the castle, but never got too close. Then one night he had a dream. He dreamed that he would find a purple flower and in the middle of the flower he would find a beautiful large pearl. He would pluck the flower and go with it to the castle. And everything that he touched with the flower would be freed from the spell. Then he dreamed that with the help of the flower Yorinde would be released and come back to him.

Next morning, as soon as he woke up, he began to search for such a flower all over the hills and dales.

He searched for eight days, then very early on the morning of the ninth day he found the purple flower and in the middle of it was a great drop of dew, just like the loveliest pearl.

Day and night he carried the flower until he came near the castle. When he was one hundred paces from the castle he was not turned to stone, but walked straight up to the door. Filled with joy, he touched the door with the flower and it trundled open. He went through the doorway and into the courtyard; then he listened for the chirping of the birds. At last he heard it, so he walked on and came to the great hall.

There in the hall was the witch, feeding the birds in the seven thousand cages. When the old witch saw Yoringel, she was furious and screamed and raved and spat out poison at him. But she couldn't come within two steps of him. He took no notice of her, but went to look closely at the cages. But there were hundreds and hundreds of nightingales. So how could he recognize Yorinde?

While he was looking, he noticed that the old woman was trying to sneak away towards the door, with a cage in her hand. So, quickly, he leapt at her and touched the cage and the old woman with his flower. Now she could no longer cast a spell on anyone!

And Yorinde stood there, freed from the spell. She embraced Yoringel and she was as beautiful as ever. Then Yoringel released all the birds from the spell and they all changed back into young girls. Then he and Yorinde went home and lived happily together for many years.

Sweet Porridge

Once there was a poor girl who lived alone with her mother, and one day they ran out of food. So the girl went off into the woods, and there she found an old woman, who already knew of her misery, and gave her a little pot. When you said, 'Cook, little pot', it produced a potful of sweet porridge. And when you said, 'Stop, little pot', it stopped and cooled off.

The little girl took the pot home to her mother, and from that day they no longer suffered from hunger: they could enjoy a meal of sweet porridge as often as they liked.

One day the girl went out. Her mother felt hungry and so she said, 'Cook, little pot.' The pot cooked a potful of porridge, and soon the mother was full and satisfied. But she had forgotten how to tell the pot to stop, so the pot just went on, cooking, and boiling, and producing hot sweet porridge. Soon the pot was full, and the porridge spilled out,

over the top, and ran over, until it filled the kitchen. Soon the whole house was full of porridge. Then the next-door house. Then the street. It looked as if it was going to fill the whole world, for nobody knew how to turn the pot off! All the people were going crazy.

Every house in the village was flooded with porridge, except for one, and then the girl came back. All she said was, 'Stop, little pot,' and the pot stopped spilling out porridge, and cooled off.

But if you want to get into that village, you'll have to eat your way through a lot of porridge!

Fortune's Three Favourites

One day an old man said to his three sons, 'I'm getting on in years and it'll not be long before I die. And so I want to make sure you are well provided for before this happens. I haven't a penny to my name, and what I'm going to give you may well seem to be of little worth. But the value of my gifts will depend on how you use them. Find a place where these things are still unknown and you should be able to make your fortunes.' So saying, he gave the eldest a cockerel, the second a scythe and the youngest a cat.

After the father's death, the eldest son went off with his cockerel, but wherever he went everybody knew the bird already. Even in the cities, people knew all about cockerels – even from a distance you could see them sitting up there on the top of the church spires and turning in the wind. And in the villages he heard plenty of them crowing away. Nobody was surprised to see a cockerel, so it didn't seem likely that he was going to make his fortune that way. But at last he managed to reach an island, where the people had never seen a cockerel. They didn't even know how to tell the time! Sure, they knew when it was morning or evening, but if they woke early, before it was light, they had no idea what time it was.

'Just look at this!' he said. 'What a splendid bird! It's got a ruby-red crown on its head and it wears spurs just like a knight on horseback. Every night it

crows three times at regular intervals and when it crows for the third time you can be sure that the sun is about to rise. But when year hear it crow during the day, you can tell that the weather's going to change.'

The people were really pleased with all this and next night they didn't sleep a wink; they all kept awake and listened with glee as the cockerel announced the time, loud and clear, at two, four and six o'clock. Then they asked him if the bird was for sale and how much he wanted for it.

'Oh! About as much gold as an ass can carry,' he answered.

'That's nothing, to pay for such a precious bird!' they all shouted at once. And they were only too pleased to give him exactly what he had asked for.

When he returned home with all his gold, his brothers were absolutely amazed and the second brother said, 'Well, I'd better go on my travels and see if I can sell my scythe for as much!'

But it didn't seem at all likely, because everywhere he went the farmers were carrying scythes on their shoulders, just like him. But at last he came to an island where the people had never seen a scythe. When their wheat was ready for harvest, they used to drag big cannons to the fields and blast the wheat out of the ground! But this was a ridiculous way of getting the harvest in, because many of the cannon balls went sailing right over the top of the wheatfields and others bashed the ears of the corn and smashed them all to smithereens. So they lost a lot of their wheat and, besides, the noise was deafening!

So the second brother went to work and he mowed the wheat so quietly and quickly that all the people could do was to stand with their mouths wide open with amazement. Then they were only too willing to pay him whatever he asked. He got a horse which was laden with gold – as much as it could carry.

Now the youngest brother was also keen to sell his cat for a good price. His journey was just like those of his brothers. As long as he stayed on the mainland, he could do nothing. Everywhere he went, people already had lots of cats. In fact there were so many, that most of the kittens were drowned at birth.

At last, he sailed over to an island, where the people had never seen a cat. The place was so overrun with mice that he found them dancing on the benches and tables. They took no notice of anyone and all the people could do was to complain. Even the king, in his castle, didn't know what to do to save himself from this plague of mice. In every corner, mice were squeaking and gnawing away at everything they could get their teeth into.

Then the youngest brother's cat started to chase the mice and in no time at all she cleared them out of some of the houses. So the people asked the king to buy this miraculous animal for the country. The king was very willing to pay any price the brother

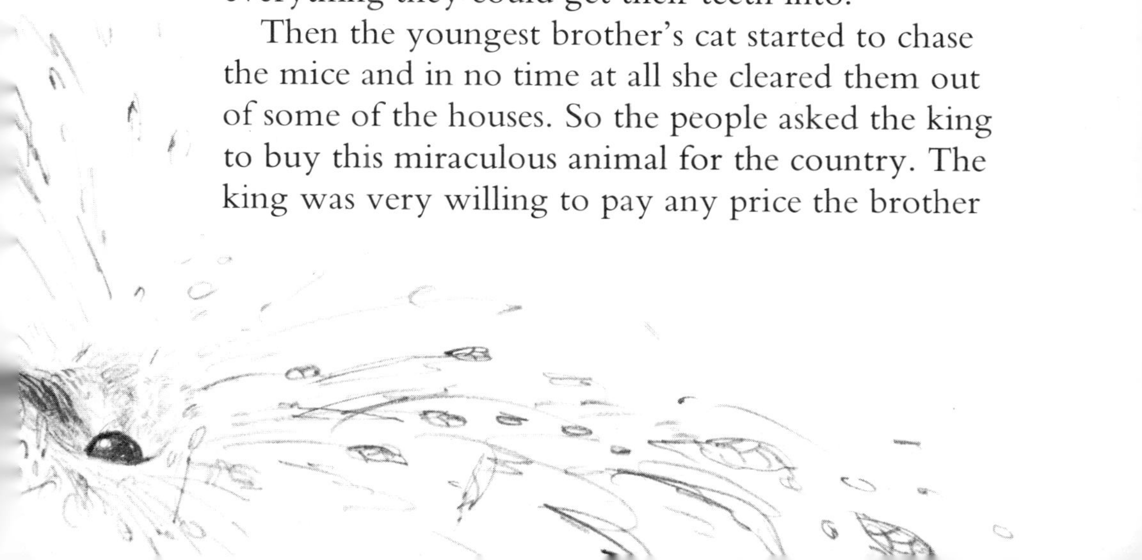

asked for, so he was paid with a mule laden with gold and when he returned home he arrived with the greatest treasure of all three.

On the island, the cat had great fun with the mice in the king's palace and killed so many that it was impossible to keep count of them. But she worked so hard that at last she became so hot and thirsty that she just stood and held her head up and cried: 'Miaow! Miaow!' The king and his household had never heard such a strange noise before and they were so terrified that they all went scrambling out of the palace. Once they were outside, the king held a meeting to decide what it was best to do. Finally, they decided to send a messenger to the cat to ask her to leave the palace. If she refused to go, then she would be in real trouble.

The King's advisers said, 'We would rather be plagued by mice than give in to such a noisy monster. At least we got used to the mice, but *this*!' So a pageboy had to go to the castle and ask the cat if she was willing to leave. But by now the cat was almost dying of thirst and simply cried 'Miaow! Miaow!'

The page thought that the answer meant, 'By no means! By no means!' and passed this message back to the King. Then the King's advisers said, 'Well, we shall just have to overpower her.' So they dragged cannons to the castle and set fire to it and shot it to pieces. When the flames reached the room where the cat was sitting, she jumped safely out of the window and left. But the cannons didn't stop firing until the whole castle was just a heap of dust!

The Old Woman in the Woods

One day a family was travelling in a carriage through a great forest. Just as they reached the middle of the forest, a band of robbers sprang out on them and murdered everybody, except the poor servant-girl who had leapt out of the carriage, terrified, and hidden behind a tree.

As soon as the robbers had run away, with all their loot, she crept out from behind the tree and saw the terrible things they had done. She began to weep, and cried, 'What shall I do now, poor girl that I am? I've no idea how to get out of this forest, for there's no one living here who can show me the way. I shall starve to death!'

She wandered around, looking for a path, but she couldn't find one. As night fell, she sat down at the foot of a tree, and decided to sit there and not move an inch, whatever happened.

After she had been sitting there for a while, a white dove came flying down to her, and in its beak it was carrying a little golden key. The bird put the key into her hand, and then it said, 'Do you see that great big tree over there? It has a little lock on it, and if you open that lock with the key you will find plenty of food and drink; and you can eat and drink as much as you like, and satisfy your hunger and your thirst.'

So the poor girl went to the tree, turned the key in the lock, and inside she found a dish full of milk,

and bread to break into it: so she could eat and satisfy her hunger.

When she was full, she said, 'This is the time when the hens at home go to bed. I'm so tired, I wish *I* had somewhere to lie down and sleep.'

Then the dove came flying down again, and brought her another golden key in its beak, and said: 'Just go and open the tree over there, and you'll find a bed.'

So the poor girl opened the tree, and inside she found a soft little bed. Then she said her prayers, lay down, and fell fast asleep.

Next morning, the dove came for the third time, and again it gave the girl a little key. 'Open the tree over there,' it said. 'Inside, you will find some clothes to wear.'

When the girl opened the tree, she found some dresses decorated with gold and jewels; they were even more beautiful than a princess's.

She lived for a long time in the wood, and every day the dove came to take care of her. It was a good, peaceful life.

But one day the dove came to her, and said, 'If you love me, will you do something for me?'

'Of course!' the girl said. 'With all my heart.'

Then the dove said, 'I'm going to show you the way to a little cottage, where an old woman lives. Go straight in, and you'll see her sitting by the fire. She will say "Good day," but you must *not* say anything. Just let her do whatever she wants; all you have to do is to go to the right, and there you'll find a door. Open it. Go into the next room, and in there you'll find a table piled high with a great heap of rings set with precious jewels. Don't touch them. Look carefully, and you will find a plain gold ring. Bring this one to me, as fast as you can.'

So the girl went to the cottage, and went straight in. There sat the old woman, with great staring eyes. And, sure enough, she said, 'Good afternoon, my child.' But the girl said nothing, and walked straight to the door on the right.

'Where are you off to?' the old woman shouted, and tried to grab her by her dress, to hold her back. 'This is my house. Nobody is allowed to come bursting in here unless I give them permission!'

But the girl said not a word, and broke away from the old woman and went into the next room. And there she saw the great heap of rings on the table, sparkling and glittering. She searched quickly for the plain gold ring but couldn't see it anywhere.

As she searched, she suddenly saw the old woman tip-toeing away, a bird-cage in her hands. So the girl rushed after her and snatched the cage from her, held it up high, and saw a bird sitting inside. And in its beak was the plain gold ring.

She snatched the ring, ran happily out of the cottage, and went to the place where she expected to meet the dove. But it wasn't there, and it didn't come.

So she waited, leaning against the tree. And the tree trunk gradually started to turn soft, and its branches began to droop. Suddenly two of the branches closed round her, and they were human arms! She turned round, and the tree had turned

into a handsome man. He held her in his arms, kissed her, and said, 'You have saved me from the power of the old woman. She is a wicked witch, who changed me into a tree. Every day for two hours I was able to change into a white dove. But as long as she had that plain gold ring, I could never become a human again.'

And as he spoke, the other trees changed back into his servants and horses. They had also been under a spell, and now they were free.

Then they all rode back to the man's kingdom, for he was a prince; the girl went with him, and married him, and they lived happily ever after.